And the
WORD
became
COLOR

And the
WORD
became
COLOR

*Exploring the Bible
with paper, pen, and paint*

DEBBY TOPLIFF

For Psalm 1 people everywhere

... *as it is written in Isaiah the prophet:*

"I will send my messenger ahead of you,
who will prepare your way" —
"a voice of one calling in the wilderness,
'Prepare the way for the Lord,
make straight paths for him.'"
—Mark 1:2-3

Contents

PART 3: Practicing Life-Long Learning: How Do We Become Like Jesus?

Introduction

Then I saw another mighty angel coming down from heaven. He was robed in a cloud, with a rainbow above his head; his face was like the sun, and his legs were like fiery pillars. He was holding a little scroll, which lay open in his hand.... Then the voice that I had heard from heaven spoke to me once more: "Go, take the scroll that lies open in the hand of the angel who is standing on the sea and on the land.".... So I went to the angel and asked him to give me the little scroll. He said to me, "Take it and eat it...."

—Revelation 10:1-9

The first time the Bible came alive to me was on the top floor of a chalet high in the Swiss Alps at a study center called L'Abri[1]. I'm not sure why I carried a pocket New Testament in my backpack because I was confused about the Bible: how could the best-selling book of all time be the most boring and unintelligible book I'd ever tried to read?

But that July evening in 1970 my life changed forever. I went to a prayer meeting where I experienced something extraordinary: I listened as people talked to God as if he were real and actually cared what they had to say. As one prayer request followed another, a sensation began to fill my body—a burning in my bones, a kindling of faith—and I, too, uttered a short request—that my life be used to help others who were lost like me.

Later that evening, back in my room, I pulled out the tiny New Testament and opened it at random to the Book of Acts, something I'd never read or known existed. As I began reading about the lives of the first Christians, the ink and paper were transformed and it was as if I was watching a movie. I could see Peter and the disciples in prison, the angel opening the door, Saul's

vision on the road to Damascus, his escape in a basket through an opening in the city wall.

When I returned home to the United States for my senior year in college, I began meeting with a small group of fellow students to study the Bible, share our experiences, and pray. I also started reading the Bible on my own. When I came to the fourth chapter of Matthew's gospel describing Jesus' temptation in the wilderness, I found a familiar phrase, "People do not live on bread alone." I had not realized it came from the mouth of Jesus who was quoting Deuteronomy 8:3 from the Old Testament. Nor did I have any idea what the rest of the verse said. What do people need in order to live? According to the Bible, people live "on every word that comes from the mouth of God".

That thought struck deep in my mind and heart. Before my encounter with God in Switzerland, my soul was starving. Now I knew where to go to feed myself. I started with a simple Bible study method called "**ABC**". I chose a short passage, then **A**nalyzed it, making a short outline to see what was actually being said. Next I chose a **B**est verse, something that spoke to me, and memorized it. Finally I made a **C**ommitment to do whatever I was learning from the passage. As I read through passages, I found many verses I didn't understand, but I looked for a morsel that made sense. There was always something I could chew on from God's vast smorgasbord!

$A.$ 1. ____ 2. ____ 3. ____

$B.$ " "

$C.$ I will . . . . .

Somewhere along the way, maybe in church, I learned that the Psalms were actually songs. One sunny fall afternoon I decided to sit on the fire escape outside my bedroom and make up a tune to the words of one of the Psalms. I've always felt a strange kinship with squirrels, and my second floor apartment in an old house put me on the same level with a squirrel nest outside my window. I used to leave peanut butter and Ritz crackers on the fire escape and watch the squirrels come up and eat. That afternoon while I sat in the sun and sang, I noticed a squirrel on the ground far below me. As I sang praises to God, the little creature climbed the stairs and sat at my feet. My soul leapt for joy as the two of us worshipped the Creator together.

After college I went to divinity school to learn more about God's Word. During that time I married and transferred to my husband's theological seminary where he was part of a group starting their own worshipping community. We took turns planning Sunday services.

One weekend, when it was our turn, my husband typed out the words of Philippians 2:1-11 to be used as a responsive reading.

If you look this up in your Bible, you'll see most of it looks like a poem. I knew from studying that scholars considered this passage to be an ancient hymn to Christ. It was a song! So I got my guitar and made up a melody to the words. This was the beginning of my writing Scripture songs. I found that if I put the words of the Bible to music, I could remember them. God's Word lived inside of me and I could pull it up in my memory when I needed it.

Sometimes the Scripture songs came to the surface on their own. One day I was driving somewhere while my baby was fussing in the back seat, traffic was terrible, and I was feeling very annoyed by another driver. All of a sudden I realized I was singing one of my songs, based on Philippians 4:5-7. *"When you're worried, when you're sad, when you're discouraged, and even when you're mad...."* Oops. I was mad. The next part of the song offered the solution I needed: *"Pray to the Lord*

in everything; tell him what you need. Give him thanks for being our God, and receive his peace."

Over the years I've been in various Bible study groups. For one stretch of time I participated in *Precepts* by Kay Arthur. Her inductive studies use workbooks that require five hours of homework a week. They're not for everyone, but I loved it. When the local church stopped offering the classes, I decided to buy the workbooks and study on my own. I chose the Book of Revelation. The last book of the Bible is arguably one of the most difficult books of Scripture to understand, and that's why I chose it; I needed help. One of the assignments was to sketch—using stick figures and simple symbols—what was happening in each chapter. I never considered myself an artist, but I found that assignment very enjoyable. In the back of my mind I thought that someday I would like to take all the sketches and put them together to create one overall picture of the whole book.

I mentioned this idea to a friend and she said, "Why don't you do it? Are you afraid it will be too hard?" I thought for a moment, because I knew it wasn't the challenge that was stopping me—I like challenges—but what was it? Then I said to her, "I'm afraid it will be too much fun!" My own words stopped me cold. Why was I waiting to have fun? So I decided right then that even if it looked like a seven-year-old did it, I would give myself permission to paint the images of Revelation on one large canvas.

I hung a five-by-seven-foot canvas on a wall in my writing studio and began to paint. I discovered it was fun, lots of fun. I ignored my inhibitions and let the little girl in me play with paint. At first I was embarrassed by my lack of skill and what I took to be crudeness in my primitive style. But when family and friends saw what I was creating, they were intrigued. I found it was a perfect storytelling tool. Even people who didn't know anything about God or the Bible were interested to hear the stories. Eventually I went on to produce a forty-five-minute video based on the painting, where I retell the story of Revelation while the images move across the screen.

Revelation was a perfect portion of Scripture to paint because the whole book—except for two chapters of letters to the seven churches—is a vision the Apostle John received while he was praying. When people asked me what book I was going to paint next, I shook my head and said I didn't think there was one I could paint.

Then I remembered what happened to me in Switzerland after the prayer meeting where I first encountered the Living God. When I randomly opened my pocket New Testament to the Book of Acts, the characters on the page were so real to me that I seemed to be watching a movie. Maybe—if I just used stick figures and didn't worry about faces—I could draw and then paint the the Book of Acts.

I began a project of studying and sketching the stories of the first Christians. My method was to read a short passage and then draw just what the Bible said. Interesting things happened as I slowed my reading down to the speed of my drawing, and tried to capture all the details. I noticed things I missed by just reading, and I found I could remember the story more easily and clearly than before.

Unlike Revelation, which is otherworldly and like a dream, Acts is an historical book reporting the adventures of real people in real time. I decided I needed to distinguish one person from another. In my painting version, I gave each significant character a different "outfit" so I could track when people came in and out of the story and interacted with each other.

Here's the sketch, and then painting, of Acts 23:12-22. It took longer than I thought it would to draw circles and then add lines to make the heads and bodies of 40 men. Drawing helped me see that forty is a lot of people![2]

High Priest

40 men
who take an oath
to kill Paul

Paul's
nephew

I give myself permission to have fun. I leave my inhibitions and the annoying internal judge outside while I go into my studio to play with paint. I don't worry about making buildings three dimensional or what the uniforms of the soldiers of the era really looked like. I concentrate on noticing what Scripture actually records and find a way to translate that into a simple picture that makes sense to me.

I coined a phrase for this new method of Bible study: "*Visual Lectio Divina*". Through the centuries Christians have practiced *Lectio Divina*,[3] a Latin phrase meaning Divine Reading. Adding the visual step of drawing what you read has the effect of emblazoning the text in your mind even more firmly, allowing you to ponder its meaning, and put it into practice in your life.

I like big projects and at this point in my life I value seeing whole books of the Bible on one large canvas. But anyone can benefit from using this method to study even a small portion of the Bible. No technical or artistic skills are necessary, just courage and attentiveness. Don't worry how it looks or what other people might think. Allow yourself to become like a little child and you will discover new dimensions to the God's Word. Dig in using your pencil or pen as a fork and spoon. Taste and see that the Lord is good.

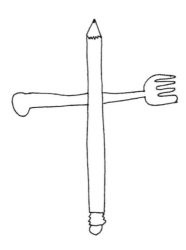

PART 1
Bringing Biblical Stories to Life

Who is Jesus?

"When the centurion, who stood there in front of Jesus, saw how he died, he said, 'Surely this man was the Son of God.'" —Mark 15:39

CHAPTER 1
Jesus is the Word of God

There are many activities we do in life, but breathing and eating are two essentials without which no one will live. I like to think of prayer as breathing. Scripture tells us to pray continually, pray without ceasing. As we practice various forms of prayer, we learn to go deeper in our relationship with God. We develop a habit of including God in all of our thoughts. We turn our worries into cries for help and our joys into thanksgiving.

Prayer is wonderful and keeps us alive. But we also need nourishment if we want to grow and become strong. Jesus quoted Deuteronomy 8:3, "People do not live on bread alone, but on every word that comes from the mouth of God."[1] Peter and Paul and the author of Hebrews all refer to God's Word as food, distinguishing between milk that babies drink, and solid food for the mature.[2]

Throughout Scripture there are strong encouragements to read and study and hide God's Word in our hearts. It is sweeter than honey, more precious than gold, protects us, and provides a great reward.[3] When we renew our minds, we are transformed and able to find God's will for our lives.[4] Knowing God's Word corrects us and equips us for all kinds of good work in the world.[5]

But the Bible can feel intimidating: sixty-six books written thousands of years ago in strange languages. How do we eat what at first might appear to be petrified crusts of bread? Can only scholars unlock the ancient texts? Are we dependent on others to plan the menu? Must we be spoon-fed? Or can we learn to feed ourselves?

Yes, I say to the last question. Not only can you find and taste the honey of God on your own, but you will have great fun doing it. So if you're hungry and humble, willing to make a mess —or create a masterpiece—get a piece of paper and a pencil and we'll begin.

Parable of the Sower

Let's start with a story Jesus told his listeners in order to help them understand the nature of God's Word. The same story is found in Matthew, Mark, and Luke.[6]

Below is Mark's version.

Here are the steps we will follow:

1. Read the passage
2. Set the scene
3. Illustrate the action / story
4. Diagram the explanation
5. Apply what we learn to our lives
6. Create a piece of art
7. Extra credit[7]

1. Read the passage

Have paper and pencil ready and feel free to take notes when something strikes you on the first reading. Because this passage of Scripture is a full twenty verses, with many visual cues, you may want to take more than one sitting to complete the exercise.

The Parable of the Sower
Mark 4:1-20

Again Jesus began to teach by the lake. The crowd that gathered around him was so large that he got into a boat and sat in it out on the lake, while all the people were along the shore at the water's edge. He taught them many things by parables, and in his teaching said: "Listen! A farmer went out to sow his seed. As he was scattering the seed, some fell along the path, and the birds came and ate it up. Some fell on rocky places, where it did not have much soil. It sprang up quickly, because the soil was shallow. But when the sun came up, the plants were scorched, and they withered because they had no root. Other seed fell among thorns, which grew up and choked the plants, so that they did not bear grain. Still other seed fell on good soil. It came up, grew and produced a crop, some multiplying thirty, some sixty, some a hundred times."

Then Jesus said, "Whoever has ears to hear, let them hear."

When he was alone, the Twelve and the others around him asked him about the parables. He told them, "The secret of the kingdom of God has been given to you. But to those on the outside everything is said in parables so that,

> "'they may be ever seeing but never perceiving,
>   and ever hearing but never understanding;
> otherwise they might turn and be forgiven!'"

Then Jesus said to them, "Don't you understand this parable? How then will you understand any parable? The farmer sows the word. Some people are like seed along the path, where the word is sown. As soon as they hear it, Satan comes and takes away the word that was sown in them. Others, like seed sown on rocky places, hear the word and at once receive it with joy. But since they have no root, they last only a short time. When trouble or persecution comes because of the word, they quickly fall away. 18 Still others, like seed sown among thorns, hear the word; but the worries of this life, the deceitfulness of wealth and the desires for other things come in and choke the word, making it unfruitful. Others, like seed sown on good soil, hear the word, accept it, and produce a crop—some thirty, some sixty, some a hundred times what was sown."

2. Set the scene

Where does this story take place?
Where is Jesus?
Who is present?

Here's how I begin. You can go about it any way you want.[8]

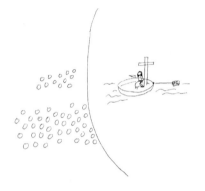

- Draw a shoreline and a simple boat.
- Put Jesus sitting in the boat. (I give him a special beard so I'll always recognize him.)
- Create the crowd by drawing their heads. (I only drew forty heads—not a big crowd, but lots of drawing!)
- Draw 12 heads for the disciples.

Next:

- Add bodies under the heads. (I draw a triangle to show people sitting.)
- Include women, children, and babies.
- Consider giving an older person a cane or a long beard.

3. Illustrate the parable (vv. 3-8)

- Draw a farmer scattering seed.
- Illustrate the four types of soil.

a. Some seed falls on the path where birds eat it up. (Try using a V or a simple sideways 3 to represent a bird.)
b. Other seed falls on rocks, then withers in the sun.
c. Some seed grows, but the plants are choked by thorns.
d. Seeds in good soil produce crops of 30, 60, and 100.

4. Diagram Jesus' explanation (vv. 14-20)

- Make a chart for the four types of soil and write in key words. (If you get stuck making the chart, see page 111 for suggestions.)

A. Some people hear the Word but Satan takes it away.
B. Others hear and receive with joy but have no root. When trouble or persecution because of the Word comes, they fall away.
C. Worries, deceitfulness of wealth, and desire for other things choke the Word and make it unfruitful.
D. Others hear the Word and accept it and produce a good crop.

Jesus Teaches about Four Types of Soil

A. Path	B. Rocks
C. Thorns	**D. Good Soil**

- Note any insights you gain from your close reading and drawing. (I just noticed that in "b" the persecution and troubles come because of the Word, and that in "d" the good soil people hear AND accept the Word.)
- Has this exercise helped you remember the passage?

5. Apply what you've learned to your life

- Choose a verse, phrase, word, or image that speaks to your life right now. What kind of soil are you? Are your roots strong? Is anything choking you or preventing you from producing a crop?
- Do you have eyes to see and ears to hear?
- What would you like to do — or not do — based on what you've learned?

6. Create a piece of art. Have fun!

- Add color to your sketch.
- Create a new picture with watercolors, paints, markers, pastels, fabric, quilting, clay, collage, legos. Decorate a cake and tell the story to your family?
- Make God's Word come alive in your own unique way.
- Share what you've learned with others, using your work as a teaching tool.

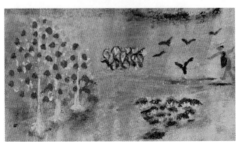

7. Extra Credit

After the Parable of the Sower in Mark 4, Jesus goes on to give three short teachings that you may want to add to your sketch book.

A Lamp on a Stand
Mark 4:21-25

He said to them, "Do you bring in a lamp to put it under a bowl or a bed? Instead, don't you put it on its stand? For whatever is hidden is meant to be disclosed, and whatever is concealed is meant to be brought out into the open. If anyone has ears to hear, let them hear."

"Consider carefully what you hear," he continued. "With the measure you use, it will be measured to you—and even more. Those who have will be given more; as for those who do not have, even what they have will be taken from them."

The Parable of the Growing Seed
Mark 4:26-29

He also said, "This is what the kingdom of God is like. A man scatters seed on the ground. Night and day, whether he sleeps or gets up, the seed sprouts and grows, though he does not know how. All by itself the soil produces grain —first the stalk, then the head, then the full kernel in the head. As soon as the grain is ripe, he puts the sickle to it, because the harvest has come."

The Parable of the Mustard Seed
Mark 4:30-34

> *Again he said, "What shall we say the kingdom of God is like, or what parable shall we use to describe it? It is like a mustard seed, which is the smallest of all seeds on earth. Yet when planted, it grows and becomes the largest of all garden plants, with such big branches that the birds can perch in its shade."*
>
> *With many similar parables Jesus spoke the word to them, as much as they could understand. He did not say anything to them without using a parable. But when he was alone with his own disciples, he explained everything.*

CHAPTER 2
Jesus is Lord of Creation

The brain is an amazing creation. It is the most complex organ in our bodies, with one hundred billion (100,000,000,000) nerve cells that produce our every thought, action, memory, feeling, and experience. The largest part of the brain (85%) is the cerebrum. The cerebrum is the thinking part of our brain and the place where our memory lives. The cerebrum has two halves and some scientists think that the right half helps us think about abstract things like music, colors, and shapes, while the left half is more analytical, helping us with math, logic, and speech.[1]

The exercises in this book combine both types of functions. We use our left brain to read and analyze the passage, then rely on our right brain to come up with creative ways to express the thoughts. I call this process *Visual Translation*. Whether your right brain is dominant, or your left, this approach to Bible study can enhance your thinking and lead you into a more imaginative and holistic experience with God's Word.

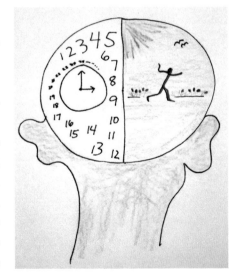

But the cerebrum also is the home of our resident critic. I'm sure you know that voice, the one that interrupts when you start to do something new, whispering, "Wait a minute, that's silly. You don't know what you're doing. You better not try that. Don't make a fool of yourself." If we want to be creative and explore new territories, we must push the mute button on our inner editor, the left side of our brain.

When I began being intentional about creative writing, I learned a wonderful trick. I set a timer for 10 minutes while I wrote on a topic. The left side of my brain was content to wait for the timer to buzz, while the right side went out on the word playground for recess. Eventually the left side editor got to do its work, but without freeing up the child living on the right side to create something fun, there would be no work to edit.

Another tactic I use to trick my inner critic into waiting quietly while I play, is to draw with pencils or crayons. I don't expect my work to look like a masterpiece when I use childlike tools. Thick and blurry lines allow for imperfections and let me concentrate on the content of my visual translation, not on its appearance. Instead of erasing or giving up and starting over, I make my mistakes work for me. Several "scribbles" of a man walking or a woman kneeling let me choose the line that best expresses my intention.

Here's the woman in Mark 5:25-34 who touches the hem of Jesus' cloak, and the same scene in my painting. It's not very realistic, but the message is clear. In the illustration on the right, the gold dots show Jesus' power going out from him.

When I finished my first large painting on the Book of Revelation, and produced the accompanying DVD, an art gallery screened the video and featured the painting on opening night. One of the visitors walked up to my painting and said, "This looks like a second grader did it." Immediately she turned to me and added, "And that's my highest compliment!" I realized I needed to embrace my inner seven-year-old! My goal is to listen to, learn from, and communicate Scripture. As I receive feedback, I realize that in God's wisdom, my lack of artistic skill is not a detriment but an asset. Often people tell me that the Book of Revelation frightened them, but seeing the images portrayed in my primitive style made John's vision much more approachable.

Calming the Storm

Let's continue our study of Mark 4 following the steps we used in chapter 1.

1. Read the passage
2. Set the scene
3. Illustrate the story
4. Diagram the teaching
5. Relate what we learn to our lives
6. Create a piece of art
7. Extra credit

1. Read the passage

In verse 35 notice that this scene takes place in the evening of the day when Jesus taught the Parable of the Sower.

Jesus Calms the Storm
Mark 4:35

> *That day when evening came, he said to his disciples, "Let us go over to the other side." Leaving the crowd behind, they took him along, just as he was, in the boat. There were also other boats with him. A furious squall came up, and the waves broke over the boat, so that it was nearly swamped. 38 Jesus was in the stern, sleeping on a cushion.[2, 3] The disciples woke him and said to him, "Teacher, don't you care if we drown?"*
>
> *He got up, rebuked the wind and said to the waves, "Quiet! Be still!" Then the wind died down and it was completely calm.*
>
> *He said to his disciples, "Why are you so afraid? Do you still have no faith?"*
>
> *They were terrified and asked each other, "Who is this? Even the wind and the waves obey him!"*

2. Set the scene

Even though this passage has only seven verses, there is a lot of action. You may want to draw more than one scene, so give yourself plenty of space to draw.

- Where does this story take place?
- Who are the characters in the story?
- How many boats are there?
- Where is Jesus?

For the first scene, I draw a line to divide the water and the sky, adding a moon and its reflection to show this takes place at night. Then I draw three boats, though there may have been more.

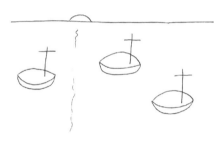

For the second scene I draw a boat rocked by waves.

The last scene is a boat on still water.

3. Illustrate the story

SCENE 1: Draw Jesus asleep in the back of one of the boats.

> • Add disciples to the boats, beginning with their heads,
>   then bodies.
> • Add sails to the boats.

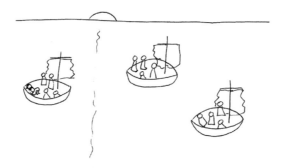

SCENE 2: Draw the disciples waking Jesus in the storm.

SCENE 3: Draw Jesus standing up, commanding the wind and the
waves to be still.

4. Diagram the teaching

One way to diagram this teaching is to make a chart with three columns: Jesus, the natural world, and the disciples. Fill in each column with what happens and what is said. (If you get stuck making the chart, see page 112 for suggestions.)

Jesus Calms the Storm

Jesus	Natural World	Disciples

- How do the disciples react in this incident?
- What do they say to each other?
- Notice how Jesus connects faith to fear.

5. Relate what you've learned to your life

- Choose a verse, phrase, word, or image that describes your life.
- Are you in a storm? Is Jesus asleep? Do you think he cares about you?
- What would Jesus say to you in your present situation?
- When someone asks you, "Who is Jesus?", how do you answer?
- Who do you go to to better understand Jesus?

6. Create a piece of art

7. Extra credit

- What do you think it means that the disciples took Jesus "just as he was"?
- Compare this passage to its parallels in Matthew and Luke listed below.
- Note new details you discover.
- How do these details add to the story?

Jesus Calms the Storm
Matthew 8:18-27

> *Then he got into the boat and his disciples followed him. Suddenly a furious storm came up on the lake, so that the waves swept over the boat. But Jesus was sleeping. The disciples went and woke him, saying, "Lord, save us! We're going to drown!"*
>
> *He replied, "You of little faith, why are you so afraid?" Then he got up and rebuked the winds and the waves, and it was completely calm.*
>
> *The men were amazed and asked, "What kind of man is this? Even the winds and the waves obey him!"*

Jesus Calms the Storm

Luke 8:22-25

> One day Jesus said to his disciples, "Let us go over to the other side of the lake." So they got into a boat and set out. As they sailed, he fell asleep. A squall came down on the lake, so that the boat was being swamped, and they were in great danger.
>
> The disciples went and woke him, saying, "Master, Master, we're going to drown!"
>
> He got up and rebuked the wind and the raging waters; the storm subsided, and all was calm. "Where is your faith?" he asked his disciples.
>
> In fear and amazement they asked one another, "Who is this? He commands even the winds and the water, and they obey him."

- Sketch Mark's account of Jesus walking on the water. Notice the reaction of the disciples.

Jesus Walks on the Water

Mark 6:45-52 [4]

> Immediately Jesus made his disciples get into the boat and go on ahead of him to Bethsaida, while he dismissed the crowd. After leaving them, he went up on a mountainside to pray.
>
> When evening came, the boat was in the middle of the lake, and he was alone on land. He saw the disciples straining at the oars, because the wind was against them. Shortly before dawn he went out to them, walking on the lake. He was about to pass by them, but when they saw him walking on the lake, they thought he was a ghost. They cried out, because they all saw him and were terrified.
>
> Immediately he spoke to them and said, "Take courage! It is I. Don't be afraid." Then he climbed into the boat with them, and the wind died down. They were completely amazed, for they had not understood about the loaves; their hearts were hardened.

CHAPTER 3

Jesus is Lord over Evil

We learn much from Scripture by asking God to open our hearts and minds, and by paying close attention to what the text says. And we can gain even more insights by using reference tools that help us place a passage within its biblical, historical, cultural, and geographic context.

There are a many different kinds of reference tools, including handbooks, concordances, Bible dictionaries, commentaries, and atlases. Study Bibles often come with introductory material at the beginning of each biblical book, notes at the side or bottom of the page, and maps and charts throughout the text and at the back. Some study Bibles stress theology, others focus on character studies, some concentrate on a special area of interest such as archeology or the Holy Spirit. Some include notes by a team of scholars, while the notes in other study Bibles are written by just one person. They come in various translations and represent a range of points of view. There are Smart Phone apps that offer all sorts of reference tools right on the screen.

Jesus and Legion

As we study the next section, Mark 5:1-20, we will incorporate information from several reference works.

1. Read the passage
2. Set the scene
3. Illustrate the story
4. See the BIG picture
5. Relate what you learn to your life
6. Create a piece of art
7. Extra credit

1. Read the passage

Jesus Restores a Demon-Possessed Man
Mark 5

They went across the lake to the region of the Gerasenes. When Jesus got out of the boat, a man with an evil spirit came from the tombs to meet him. This man lived in the tombs, and no one could bind him anymore, not even with a chain. For he had often been chained hand and foot, but he tore the chains apart and broke the irons on his feet. No one was strong enough to subdue him. Night and day among the tombs and in the hills he would cry out and cut himself with stones. When he saw Jesus from a distance, he ran and fell on his knees in front of him. He shouted at the top of his voice, "What do you want with me, Jesus, Son of the Most High God? In God's name don't torture me!" For Jesus had said to him, "Come out of this man, you evil spirit!"

Then Jesus asked him, "What is your name?"

"My name is Legion," he replied, "for we are many." And he begged Jesus again and again not to send them out of the area.

A large herd of pigs was feeding on the nearby hillside. The demons begged Jesus, "Send us among the pigs; allow us to go into them." He gave them permission, and the evil spirits came out and went into the pigs. The herd, about two thousand in number, rushed down the steep bank into the lake and were drowned. Those tending the pigs ran off and reported this in the town and countryside, and the people went out to see what had happened. When they came to Jesus, they saw the man who had been possessed by the legion of demons, sitting there, dressed and in his right mind; and they were afraid. Those who had seen it told the people what had happened to the demon-possessed man—and told about the pigs as well. Then the people began to plead with Jesus to leave their region.

As Jesus was getting into the boat, the man who had been demon-possessed begged to go with him. Jesus did not let him, but said, "Go home to your own people and tell them how much the Lord has done for you, and how he has had mercy on you." So the man went away and began to tell in the Decapolis how much Jesus had done for him. And all the people were amazed.

It is easy to determine the immediate context of Mark 5. Remember what was happening in the end of Mark 4. After teaching the Parable of the Sower, and then calming the storm, Jesus and the disciples continue to the other side of the lake.[1] In Mark 5:1 we find them landing in the region of the Gerasenes[2] which scholars think could be the city of Kursi on the map to the right. This is because at Kursi the shore is level and a good place to land a boat. About a mile

away is a steep slope within forty yards of the shore,[3] and two miles from there are cavern tombs where people used to live. The geography and landscape fit perfectly with the scene of our story.

The light green area in the map to the left is called the Decapolis (v. 20) and refers to "ten cities" founded by the Greeks and then taken over by the Romans. The Jews in Jesus' day considered the people who lived there to be pagans: they did not

believe in the God of the Bible. The Jews stayed away from the Decapolis, and called the people "unclean." Rules in the Old Testament forbid Jews from eating pork, whereas pagans not only ate pork, but sacrificed pigs in their religious ceremonies. What was sacred to the pagans was offensive to the Jews.

2. Set the scene

This is a complicated story with several scenes so give yourself plenty of room to spread out on the page. Don't worry if your drawing does not look realistic. The goal of this exercise is for you to notice the details and transfer them to your sketch book in a way that will help you remember—and understand—the story.

- Draw a shoreline where the disciples land their boat carrying Jesus.
- Draw caves or tombs where the man with the evil spirit lives.
- Create a hillside with a steep cliff where the pigs are feeding.
- Draw a town in the distance.

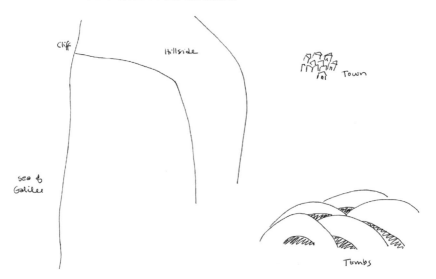

3. Illustrate the story

Because this story is full of action, you can either draw separate "scenes" like we did with the boats and the storm in chapter 2, or you can put action into more than one spot in one drawing. Start with heads, then add bodies—or whatever method works for you. Give Jesus and the man from the tombs distinguishing characteristics.

46

- Draw the boat and the disciples on the shore.
- Show Legion coming out of the tombs. Include as many details from the story as you can. What are on his hands and feet? His skin? What might you reasonably conclude from verse 15?
- Draw Legion on his knees in front of Jesus.
- Show the pigs feeding on the hillside. How many are there? Who is with the pigs?
- Think of a way to show the evil spirits coming out of Legion and going into the pigs.
- Show what happens to the pigs.
- Draw Jesus and the man who is now free. What is the man doing?
- Show the townspeople and pig herders gathering. Notice their reaction to what has happened to the man from the tombs.
- Draw the last scene, verses 18-20.

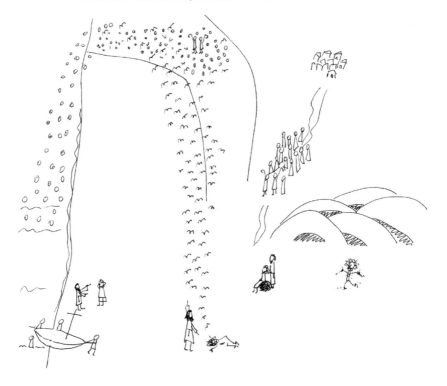

4. See the BIG Picture

In lessons 1-3 we have been following Jesus and his disciples over a two-day period. He starts on the west side of the Sea of Galilee and teaches the crowds what happens when you sow seeds in different kinds of soil. Then, in private, he explains to the disciples the meaning of the parable: the seed is the Word of God. Immediately that evening Jesus and the disciples get in a boat to sail to the east side of the lake. The wind and waves nearly swamp them, but Jesus demonstrates his power over the forces of nature.

After Jesus calms the storm, they land in the Decapolis, a region the Jews consider unclean. Jesus is met by a man with an evil spirit. This time Jesus demonstrates his power over the invisible, spiritual forces.

- Compare what happens to the wind and waves to what happens to the man.
- Compare the reaction of the disciples in the boats in Mark 4 to the reaction of the townspeople on land in Mark 5.
- What does Jesus tell the man to do in 5:19?
- What does he actually do? See verse 20.

Look at all of your sketches of this two-day time period in the life of Jesus, from the Parable of the Sower to the Demon-Possessed Man.

- Do you see connections? Is there a theme building?
- Is it possible Jesus sailed to the Decapolis because he considered it to be "Good Soil"?

Mark relates one other instance when Jesus goes to the region of the Decapolis. Read Mark 7:31-8:11 and notice what happens in this region.

Jesus Heals a Deaf and Mute Man[4]
Mark 7:31-37

Then Jesus left the vicinity of Tyre and went through Sidon, down to the Sea of Galilee and into the region of the Decapolis. There some people brought to him a man who was deaf and could hardly talk, and they begged Jesus to place his hand on him.

After he took him aside, away from the crowd, Jesus put his fingers into the man's ears. Then he spit and touched the man's tongue. He looked up to heaven and with a deep sigh said to him, "Ephphatha!" (which means "Be opened!"). At this, the man's ears were opened, his tongue was loosened and he began to speak plainly.

Jesus commanded them not to tell anyone. But the more he did so, the more they kept talking about it. People were overwhelmed with amazement. "He has done everything well," they said. "He even makes the deaf hear and the mute speak."

Jesus Feeds the Four Thousand
Mark 8:1-10

During those days another large crowd gathered. Since they had nothing to eat, Jesus called his disciples to him and said, "I have compassion for these people; they have already been with me three days and have nothing to eat. If I send them home hungry, they will collapse on the way, because some of them have come a long distance."

His disciples answered, "But where in this remote place can anyone get enough bread to feed them?"

"How many loaves do you have?" Jesus asked.

"Seven," they replied.

He told the crowd to sit down on the ground. When he had taken the seven loaves and given thanks, he broke them and gave them to his disciples to set before the people, and they did so. They had a few small fish as well; he gave thanks for them also and told the disciples to distribute them. The people ate and were satisfied. Afterward the

*disciples picked up seven basketfuls of broken pieces
that were left over. About four thousand were present.
And having sent them away, he got into the boat with his
disciples and went to the region of Dalmanutha.*

- Recall the conversation between Jesus and the man from the tombs in 5:18-20.
- What evidence do you see of seed planted in good soil?

5. Relate what you've learned to your life

- Are there people or places you avoid because you consider them to be unclean?
- Which person or group of people do you most closely identify with in Mark 5:1-20?
- Do you ever feel chained? By whom or what?
- Are you ever tempted to hurt yourself?
- Do you believe Jesus can set people free?
- What is your response when you see a demonstration of God's power?
- Is God calling you to "plant seed" in an unusual type of soil?

6. Create a piece of art

7. Extra credit

There are two miraculous feedings in Mark's gospel: the feeding of the 4,000 in Mark 8:1-10 which we just read, and the feeding of the 5,000 in Mark 6:30-45. Read both passages and fill in the chart below. (If you get stuck making the chart, see page 113 for suggestions.)

Jesus Feeds the Five Thousand[5]
Mark 6:30-35

The apostles gathered around Jesus and reported to him all they had done and taught. Then, because so many people were coming and going that they did not even have a chance to eat, he said to them, "Come with me by yourselves to a quiet place and get some rest."

So they went away by themselves in a boat to a solitary place. But many who saw them leaving recognized them and ran on foot from all the towns and got there ahead of them. When Jesus landed and saw a large crowd, he had compassion on them, because they were like sheep without a shepherd. So he began teaching them many things.

By this time it was late in the day, so his disciples came to him.

"This is a remote place," they said, "and it's already very late. Send the people away so that they can go to the surrounding countryside and villages and buy themselves something to eat."

But he answered, "You give them something to eat."

They said to him, "That would take almost a year's wages! Are we to go and spend that much on bread and give it to them to eat?"

"How many loaves do you have?" he asked. "Go and see."

When they found out, they said, "Five—and two fish."

When Jesus directed them to have all the people sit down in groups on the green grass. So they sat down in groups of hundreds and fifties. Taking the five loaves and the two fish and looking up to heaven, he gave thanks and broke the loaves. Then he gave them to his disciples to set before the people. He also divided the two fish among them all. They all ate and were satisfied, and the disciples picked up twelve basketfuls of broken pieces of bread and fish. The number of the men who had eaten was five thousand. Immediately Jesus made his disciples get into the boat and go on ahead of him to Bethsaida, while he dismissed the crowd.

Jesus Feeds the 4,000 and 5,000

	Mark 6:30-45	Mark 8:1-11
Where does the feeding take place?		
How does Jesus feel toward the people?		
How much food does Jesus start with?		
How much food is left over?		
How many people were fed?		

- What do these events tell you about Jesus?
- Some scholars see symbolic significance in the number of basketfuls left over. The twelve leftover in the feeding in Galilee, home of the Jews, could represent God's provision for all twelve tribes of Israel. The seven leftover in the Decapolis, a pagan region, could represent God's provision for the non-Jews. In Acts 13:19 and Joshua 3:10 the non-Jews are summarized by seven nations.

Below is a portion of the story of Jesus and Legion as it appears in my painting of Mark's gospel. In the lower right corner see Legion sitting with Jesus—dressed and in his right mind.

CHAPTER 4
Jesus is the Son of God

At the time of Jesus, in the region of Galilee where he lived, both boys and girls went to school until the age of thirteen. Their textbook was the Torah, the first five books of the Old Testament. By age thirteen they memorized the whole thing: the books we call Genesis, Exodus, Leviticus, Numbers, and Deuteronomy. The boys who who were recognized as spiritual leaders continued to study with a rabbi and memorize the rest of the Old Testament. I know a few people who have memorized whole books of the Bible, but the whole Bible? Wow.

In the New Testament, when one of the writers quotes part of a chapter or verse, their audience would remember the context and automatically complete the passage in their mind. If I say, "an apple a day ... " or "a stitch in time ... " you know what follows, providing you grew up in the same culture I did. I'm sure each societal group has its own collective memory.

But knowing what the Bible says does not guarantee you understand what it means—or that you let it influence your behavior and form your character.[1] In fact, it is not uncommon for Scripture to be used against God's purposes instead of for them. Our next passage illustrates this point.

All three of the synoptic gospels[2] report that after his baptism, Jesus was led (or *driven*, according to Mark) by the Holy Spirit into the desert where he was tempted by the devil for forty days. Our next exercise is to sketch what happens to Jesus and how he handles his temptation.

In order to better understand the temptation passage, we must look carefully at the biblical context—the verses just preceding the section. It is always good, when you begin reading or

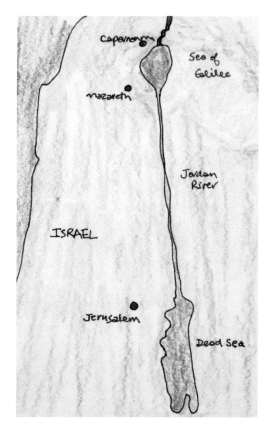

studying the Bible, to orient yourself to what has gone before. We don't want to misuse God's Word!

Matthew 3:13 says that Jesus came from Galilee to the Jordan River to be baptized by John. The map to the left shows the broader region of Israel, with Galilee on the edge of the Sea of Galilee in the north. Jerusalem, the capitol, is west of the north end of the Dead Sea.

Jesus' Temptation

1. Read the passage
2. Set the scene
3. Illustrate the story
4. Analyze the teaching
5. Relate what we learn to your life
6. Create a piece of art
7. Extra credit

1. Read the passage

Matthew 3:16-4:11

Jesus Tested in the Wilderness

As soon as Jesus was baptized, he went up out of the water. At that moment heaven was opened, and he saw the Spirit of God descending like a dove and alighting on him. And a voice from heaven said, "This is my Son, whom I love; with him I am well pleased."

Then Jesus was led by the Spirit into the wilderness to be tempted by the devil. After fasting forty days and nights, he was hungry. The tempter came to him and said, "If you are the Son of God, tell these stones to become bread."

Jesus answered, "It is written: 'People do not live on bread alone, but on every word that comes from the mouth of God.'"

Then the devil took him to the holy city and had him stand on the highest point of the temple.[3] "If you are the Son of God," he said, "throw yourself down. For it is written:

"'He will command his angels concerning you,
and they will lift you up in their hands,
so that you will not strike your foot against a stone.'"

Jesus answered him, "It is also written: 'Do not put the Lord your God to the test.'"

Again, the devil took him to a very high mountain and showed him all the kingdoms of the world and their splendor. "All this I will give you," he said, "if you will bow down and worship me."

Jesus said to him, "Away from me, Satan! For it is written: 'Worship the Lord your God, and serve him only.'"

Then the devil left him, and angels came and attended him.

2. Set the scenes

There are 6 different scenes or actions in the above passage. I separated the sections with a space to make it easier for you. Depending on the paper you use, divide your work area into six squares. If you are using a loose sheet of paper, you can fold in half and then thirds.

- SCENE 1: Draw a river with Jesus standing on the side of it.
- SCENE 2: Show Jesus walking into the wilderness.
- SCENE 3: Draw some stones. Have Jesus sitting on one of them.
- SCENE 4: Draw a tall building with Jesus standing on the top.
- SCENE 5: Show Jesus standing on top of a mountain.
- SCENE 6: Draw scene 3 again.

3. Illustrate the story

The rest of the "characters" in the story are beings who are usually invisible to us. Use your imagination in drawing the Spirit, the devil, and angels.

- SCENE 1: Add the Spirit of God descending or alighting on Jesus.
- SCENE 2: Add the Spirit leading Jesus into the wilderness.
- SCENE 3: Show the devil talking to Jesus. Make some indication of 40 days.
- SCENE 4: Put the devil on top of the Temple with Jesus.
- SCENE 5: Put Satan on the mountain top with Jesus. Indicate Jesus telling Satan to go away.
- SCENE 6: Show angels attending to Jesus.

4. Analyze the Teaching

There's something missing from our sketches — the dialogue! Fill in the chart below noting each scene. Write down the name of the speaker or speakers, or who creates the action. Note what has just happened prior to the words or actions. Fill in what is said or what happens. If the words are a quotation from Scripture, note the reference. Most Bibles have footnotes telling the reference. (If you get stuck making the chart, see pages 112-113 for suggestions.)

Jesus is Tested in the Wilderness

Scene	Speaker or Actor	Situation	
1	A voice from heaven		
2	The Spirit		
3	Tempter		
	Jesus		
4	The devil		
	Jesus		
5	The devil		
	Jesus		
6	Angels		

This is a rich and fascinating passage. We created a picture with the right side of our brain of what was happening to Jesus. Now we can use the left side of our brain to analyze it.

- How many "actors" are in this portion of Scripture?
- SCENE 1: Who are these words addressed to? What is the speaker's relationship to Jesus?
- SCENE 2: Describe the relationship between Jesus and the Spirit.
- SCENE 3: How is Jesus feeling when the temptation begins? How do the words of the devil compare to the words from heaven? What does Jesus use to counteract the temptation?

	Words Spoken or Actions Taken	Reference

- SCENE 4: Compare Jesus' defense in scene 3 with the devil's second attack. Are you surprised that the devil quotes Scripture? Is the promise from Psalm 91 fulfilled elsewhere in the passage?
- SCENE 5: According to this passage, who is in charge of all the kingdoms of the world? Does this surprise you? How does Jesus address the devil? What did Jesus tell him to do? How many names is he called by in this passage?
- SCENE 6: Did the devil obey Jesus? Imagine what it might be like to be attended to by angels. Consider the quotation from Psalm 91.

5. Relate what you've learned to your life

This passage is where I first discovered the answer to the familiar quotation about not living by bread alone. Although Jesus said it, he was quoting Moses in Deuteronomy 8:3. Throughout this passage we see that Jesus puts himself under the authority of Scripture. The word of God is not only his food, but also the tool he uses to resist the temptations of the devil.

- How would you describe your relationship to the Spirit of God?
- Who or what defines your identity?
- Consider Jesus' physical state when the devil first approached him. When are you most vulnerable?[4] What do you hunger for?
- What things do you think you must have in order to live a full life? A spouse? Children? An important job? Good health? Excitement?
- The second temptation is tricky because the devil quotes Scripture and states says something that is true. What do you think it means to put God to the test? Are there ways you try to test God's faithfulness?
- In the Parable of the Sower that we studied in chapter 1, Jesus taught about different kinds of soil. Review the chart on page 28 and compare the three temptations of Jesus

with the things that threaten the seed (the Word of God) from being fruitful.
- What "splendorous" things—wealth, fame, power— tempt you to forsake your allegiance to God?
- Are there any instances when Satan has snatched the Word of God away from you? How can you protect yourself?

6. Create a piece of art

- Go to a beach or a park that has a sandy area and re-enact the scenes of Jesus' temptation using natural objects like stones and twigs and leaves to represent the elements of the story.

7. Extra credit

- Compare our passage in Matthew with its parallel in Luke 4:1-13. Note any differences between them.
- Pay particular attention to Luke 4:5-7. What does this expanded version tell us about the devil? What do we learn from 4:13?

Luke 4:1-13

Jesus, full of the Holy Spirit, left the Jordan and was led by the Spirit into the wilderness, where for forty days he was tempted by the devil. He ate nothing during those days, and at the end of them he was hungry.

The devil said to him, "If you are the Son of God, tell this stone to become bread."

Jesus answered, "It is written: 'People do not live on bread alone.'"

The devil led him up to a high place and showed him in an instant all the kingdoms of the world. And he said to him, "I will give you all their authority and splendor; it has been given to me, and I can give it to anyone I want to. If you worship me, it will all be yours."

Jesus answered, "It is written: 'Worship the Lord your God and serve him only.'"

The devil led him to Jerusalem and had him stand on the highest point of the temple. "If you are the Son of God," he said, "throw yourself down from here. For it is written:

"'He will command his angels concerning you
to guard you carefully;
they will lift you up in their hands,
so that you will not strike your foot against a stone.'"

Jesus answered, "It is said: 'Do not put the Lord your God to the test.'"

When the devil had finished all this tempting, he left him until an opportune time.

• Read Mark's account of the temptation in 1:12-13. Although brief, what additional information does he include?

Mark 1:12-13

At once the Spirit sent him out into the wilderness, and he was in the wilderness forty days, being tempted by Satan. He was with the wild animals, and angels attended him.

Often people comment that the bad or wicked characters in a novel or movie are more interesting than the "good" characters. If that is true, then the fault lies with the creator of the story. In my life I have noticed that evil is not very creative, but employs the same tactics over and over. When you have experienced it enough, you begin to recognize the patterns. God, on the other hand, is infinitely creative. Throughout the Scripture God proclaims, "See I am doing a new thing. . . . I make all things new."[5]

In all three of the Gospel passages describing Jesus' testing, a voice from heaven announces that Jesus is God's Son. The devil's ploy in the first two temptations is to question the truth of that statement. This is the same tactic he used on Adam and Eve in the Garden of Eden. Read Genesis 2:15-3:1-5, being careful to note exactly what God says and who he says it to, the serpent's question to Eve, and her recollection of God's command (which according to the account, was given to Adam before Eve was created.)

Genesis 2:15-3:5

> The LORD God took the man and put him in the Garden of Eden to work it and take care of it. And the LORD God commanded the man, "You are free to eat from any tree in the garden; but you must not eat from the tree of the knowledge of good and evil, for when you eat of it you will certainly die."
>
> The LORD God said, "It is not good for the man to be alone. I will make a helper suitable for him."...
>
> So the LORD God caused the man to fall into a deep sleep; and while he was sleeping, he took one of the man's ribs and then closed up the place with flesh. Then the LORD God made a woman from the rib he had taken out of the man, and he brought her to the man....
>
> Now the serpent was more crafty than any of the wild animals the LORD God had made. He said to the woman, "Did God really say, 'You must not eat from any tree in the garden'?"
>
> The woman said to the serpent, "We may eat fruit from the trees in the garden, but God did say, 'You must not eat fruit from the tree that is in the middle of the garden, and you must not touch it, or you will die.'"
>
> You will not certainly die," the serpent said to the woman. "For God knows that when you eat of it your eyes will be opened, and you will be like God, knowing good and evil."

- There are several places in the Bible where evil is personified. In addition to the Book of Revelation and Job 1 and 2, consider the following:

1 Chronicles 21:1

> Satan rose up against Israel and incited David to take a census of Israel.

Zechariah 3:1
> Then he showed me Joshua the high priest standing before the angel of the LORD, and Satan standing at his right side to accuse him.

Isaiah 14:12-15
> How you have fallen from heaven,
>   morning star, son of the dawn!
> You have been cast down to the earth,
>   you who once laid low the nations!
> You said in your heart,
>   "I will ascend to heaven;
> I will raise my throne
>   above the stars of God;
> I will sit enthroned on the mount of assembly,
>   on the utmost heights of Mount Zaphon.
> I will ascend above the tops of the clouds;
>   I will make myself like the Most High."
> But you are brought down to the realm of the dead,
>   to the depths of the pit.

Luke 10:18-20
> He replied, "I saw Satan fall like lightning from heaven. I have given you authority to trample on snakes and scorpions and to overcome all the power of the enemy; nothing will harm you. However, do not rejoice that the spirits submit to you, but rejoice that your names are written in heaven."

2 Corinthians 11
> Satan himself masquerades as an angel of light. It is not surprising, then, if his servants also masquerade as servants of righteousness. Their end will be what their actions deserve.

How Do We Follow Jesus?

"'Come follow me,' Jesus said, 'and I will send you out to catch people.' At once they left their nets and followed him." —Mark 1:17-18

CHAPTER 5

Growing in God

In the first four chapters we explored the process of visual Bible study with passages that tell a story so we were able to set the scene, draw the characters, discover and illustrate the details, and capture the dynamic of the biblical drama. The Old Testament abounds with such stories, from creation to the family of Abraham, the life of Moses and the Exodus of God's people from Egypt, the period of the judges, and the long reign of kings. Sections of the prophetic books make good sources for sketching and painting, especially their visions and metaphorical language.

In the New Testament, as we have seen, the four gospels are full of stories and parables perfect for visual study. The Book of Acts—the history of the early church—contains over 100 vignettes featuring important historical figures such as Peter, Paul, Barnabas, Stephen, and many others. John's extensive vision in the Book of Revelation becomes much more approachable and understandable through visual Bible study.

Yet much of the Bible is practical instruction and theological teaching. I've found that using paper and pencil—along with my imagination—helps me think through some of the left-brain ideas and find an image or pattern on which I can hang my thoughts and aid my memory.

Over the years I have learned a few helpful "tricks" that make studying the Bible more fun for me. My first breakthrough was when my husband came home from a business trip to the UK and brought me an inexpensive paperback Bible—with a beautiful Monet painting on the cover. I decided that since it did not have gold leaf pages bound in leather, it was okay for me to mark up the pages. Then I bought a fine-line micro pigment pen with waterproof ink, available in black and colors.

As I read passages, I make notations of anything that catches my attention. I underline verses, double underline words or phrases that are repeated. I circle key words or ideas, make stars in the margin, etc. I draw lines across the page to connect similar thoughts and draw simple icons above or on top of certain words.

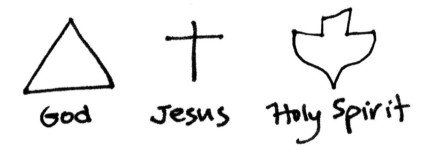

From "playing within the test" I moved to drawing in the margins and the white spaces above and below the text.

Beginning here, and in the next few chapters, I will share some of my "theological" drawings. I have chosen portions of Scripture I find particularly helpful in my relationship with God. As with the story drawings we have already done, I encourage you to make your own illustrations or designs from these passages to help you ponder and remember what Scripture teaches.

1. Read the passage
2. Diagram or illustrate the concepts
3. Consider the meaning and apply what you learn to your life
4. Add color or some other creative touch

Growing in Love

Peter, one of Jesus' three closest disciples, wrote two letters included in the New Testament. In 2 Peter 1:3-4 he writes that God has given us everything we need to live a godly life and participate in the divine nature. In the next verses Peter explains how we can progress into a life of maturity.

1. Read the passage

2 Peter 1:5-7

> *For this very reason, make every effort to add to your faith goodness; and to goodness, knowledge; and to knowledge, self-control; and to self-control, perseverance; and to perseverance, godliness; and to godliness, mutual affection; and to mutual affection, love.*

2. Diagram or illustrate the concepts

You could draw this as a mathematical equation, adding all the elements that yield a godly life:

faith + goodness + knowledge + self-control + perseverance
+ godliness + mutual affection + love = godly life.

Or you could separate the qualities into "attitudes" and "actions". (If you get stuck making the chart, see page 114 for suggestions.)

Attitudes and Actions in 2 Peter 1:5-7

Attitude	Action

I chose to draw all the characteristics as a flower:

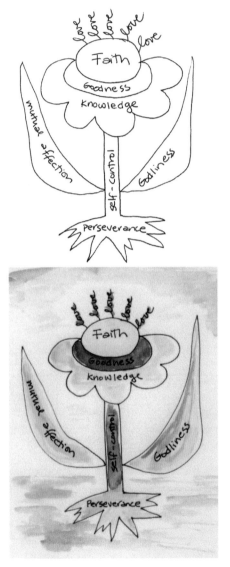

- Illustrate this passage with a design of your own. The purpose is not to come up with a beautiful drawing or clever design, but to put this teaching on paper so you can understand, remember, and apply it to your life.

3. Consider the meaning and apply what you learn to your life

- Which of these qualities are your strengths? Your weaknesses?
- How might one attitude lead to an action, and that action lead to the following attitude?
- Choose a quality you want to add to your life this week.

4. Add color or some other creative touch to your drawing

- Create your own visual version of this passage.

Finding God's Will

A few years ago my husband and I did a Bible study together on 1 Thessalonians. Each week we read a short passage and talked about it together. When we got to the very end of the book with only ten or so verses left, I skimmed them and said, "We can probably skip this part." But he thought we should take a look anyway. I was so surprised when I read the sentence that makes up 1 Thessalonians 5:16-18. Not only are verses 16 and 17 among the shortest verses in the whole Bible (two words each), but they answer a question that people ask over and over again: What is God's will for me? Although these verses don't tell you who to marry or where to live or what kind of job you should have, they set you on a course where you can discover specific direction for your life.

1. Read the passage

1 Thessalonians 5:16-18

Rejoice always, 17 pray continually, 18 give thanks in all circumstances; for this is God's will for you in Christ Jesus.

2. Diagram or illustrate the concepts

Below is one metaphor that occurred to me. Think of other ways to "picture" these verses that will help you keep them in your mind.

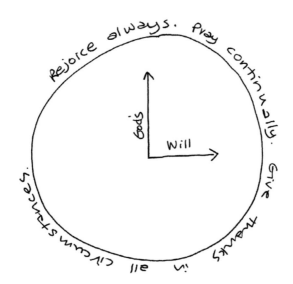

3. Consider the meaning and apply what you learn to your life

- Notice the order of these three commands. What do you usually do first?
- What kind of difference would it make in your daily life if you obeyed these directives?
- Make a list of seven things you are thankful for.

4. Add color or some other creative touch to your drawing

- Create your own visual version of this passage. (I wrote it freehand on the wall around the mirror in my studio.)

Living by the Spirit

Paul, who wrote this letter to the Thessalonians, did not have an easy life. According to his own account,[1] he was imprisoned, flogged, exposed to death, beaten with rods, stoned three times, shipwrecked, in danger from rivers, bandits, from his own people (the Jews), from Gentiles, and from false believers. He went without sleep or food water, and was cold and naked. Yet he learned to be content in every circumstance[2] and discovered the secret of rejoicing always.[3]

In his letter to the Galatians, Paul describes a person who is able to rejoice, pray, and give thanks as someone who "lives by the Spirit." He contrasts the Spirit-led life to a life controlled by our sinful nature. Take a closer look at these two ways of life.

1. Read the passage

Acts of the sinful nature:

Galatians 5:19-21

> *The acts of the sinful nature are obvious: sexual immorality, impurity and debauchery; idolatry and witchcraft;[4] hatred, discord, jealousy, fits of rage, selfish ambition, dissensions, factions and envy; drunkenness, orgies, and the like. I warn you, as I did before, that those who live like this will not inherit the kingdom of God.*

As I read through Paul's list of characteristics of the acts of the sinful nature, it reminds me of the rocky ground in the Parable of the Sower.

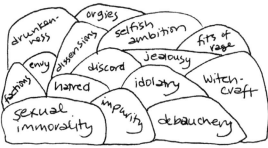

Fruit of the Spirit:

Galatians 5:22-23

> *But the fruit of the Spirit is love, joy, peace, patience, kindness, goodness, faithfulness, gentleness and self-control. Against such things there is no law.*

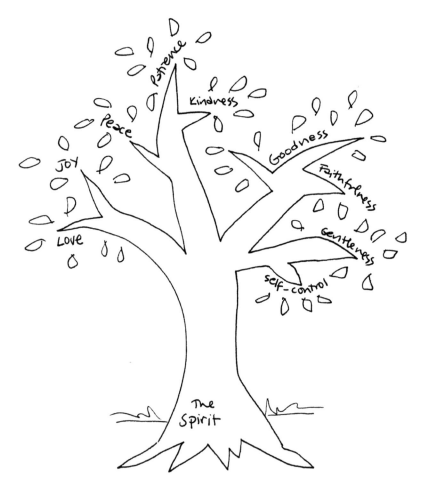

Fruit connotes something living and growing—like the seed planted in the good soil in the Parable of the Sower. Notice that the word "fruit" is singular. All nine character traits grow and mature at the same time.

2. Diagram or illustrate the concepts

- Draw your own interpretation of these two passages.
- I painted a floor cloth (acrylic on canvas then shellacked) with symbols of the fruit of the Spirit. It's still in front of my kitchen sink fifteen years later.

3. Consider the meaning and apply what you learn to your life

- Which acts of the sinful nature trouble you?
- Can you see the fruit of the Spirit growing in your character? Which ones are the most and least ripe?
- Contemplate the nature of fruit: Where does it come from? How does it grow? How does it look? Smell? What is it used for? How does it reproduce? Relate your thoughts to spiritual fruit.

4. Add color or some other creative touch to your drawing

At the end of the Book of Revelation, after death and evil have been destroyed, John the Apostle sees a new heaven and new earth, with a Holy City coming down from God.

Revelation 22:1-2

> *Then the angel showed me the river of the water of life, as clear as crystal, flowing from the throne of God and of the Lamb down the middle of the great street of the city. On each side of the river stood the tree of life, bearing twelve crops of fruit, yielding its fruit every month. And the leaves of the tree are for the healing of the nations.*

- Notice what grows on the sides of the river.
- What might these twelve crops of fruit be?
- How could the fruit of the Spirit be used in the healing of the nations?

As you read through the Bible you will find many passages about growing in God. This is the goal of all of the biblical writers —to help us learn to love God and love people. Consider keeping a personal visual journal to record what you discover about the process of spiritual growth. Make drawings and charts to help you delve into the mysteries of how God transforms our character into a beautiful flower or a flourishing tree of life.

CHAPTER 6
Living in the World

After my encounter with God in Switzerland, I had one more year of university back home in America. I found that not only had my mind been opened to the living nature of the Bible, but all my studies took on new and vivid meaning. In a class on John Milton, the 17th century poet, I read *Paradise Lost*. Like Shakespeare, William Blake, and scores of other great writers, I saw that Bible stories and teachings ran through his writing like an underground stream, bubbling up to the surface, feeding the characters and dialogue, and driving the plot.

After graduating from college, I wanted to learn more about my faith, so I went to divinity school to study the Bible. Unlike most of my classmates who had grown up in churches that taught Scripture, I was being exposed to many Bible stories for the first time. It was thrilling to experience new doors of knowledge opening before me.

During divinity school I was married, and after we graduated my husband and I helped plant a church that we called an intentional Christian community. I had many opportunities to teach and explore ways to put my love of the Bible into creative forms. I wrote songs and poems, performed liturgical dances and skits, and designed worship banners.

Somewhere along the way my strong left brain started taking over. When I read a passage, I could not stop thinking about it in analytical ways. I tripped over my own thoughts and lost my ability to see God and myself in the story. The Bible became a dry crust instead of a ripe peach. After ten years living in a Christian community, my sense of calling dwindled and I was restless.

To help me in this difficult and uncomfortable time, I found a spiritual director, a Roman Catholic sister trained to listen and respond, who met with me regularly and assigned passages for me to read and reflect on. She taught me to identify myself with the characters and imagine myself in the story. Rather than simply analyzing the meaning, she gave me permission to ask and tell God anything at all; nothing was off limits.

Even though we had three children ages two, five, and eight, my husband arranged to give me time and space in the morning to read and write in my journal. His work as manager of the local Christian bookstore two blocks from our house did not begin until 9:30 am, so he got the children up, dressed, fed, and the two older ones off to school. All three of them still think that is a father's job!

This was a time of radical change in my life. My journal filled with questions and complaints. After several months I did not seem to be making progress, until one afternoon my husband showed up unexpectedly during my spiritual direction meeting. A classmate from divinity school had called him at the bookstore and offered him a job in another city. Even though any mention of leaving our church felt taboo, I could not stop smiling. My body knew more than my brain.

That night both my husband and I came down with a terrible case of the flu. It kept us in bed for ten days while our young children opened cans of soup for dinner. As we tossed and turned in a feverish state, then gradually recovered our health, the seed idea of making a change was firmly planted and grew roots. When I fully recovered, I opened my journal and saw that my questions were answered by this new job opportunity. God works in mysterious ways in the lives of those who seek his will. Start with prayer, add people of wise counsel, search the Scriptures, and give God space and time.

There are different seasons in the spiritual life just as there are in nature. Seeds are planted and sprout in the spring, fruit grows in the summer and matures in the fall. But winter—if you live in a four-season climate—inevitably comes, and with it a time of dormancy and preparation for more growth the next spring. God provides us with tools and equipment to keep us safe and ready for whatever comes next. In this chapter we will look at Scripture passages that help us remain strong and secure as we live out our faith in the world.

Putting on God's Protection

Several years ago I attended a conference on prayer. One of the leaders taught us something I had never practiced before. He showed us how to "put on" the armor of God. In the letter to the Ephesians, Paul uses the metaphor[1] of a soldier dressed in armor. He likens physical equipment used in warfare to the spiritual gifts of God that protect us in spiritual battles. At the conference we went through motions of taking up all the elements of armor and putting them in place on our own bodies.

1. Read the passage
2. Diagram or illustrate the concepts
3. Consider the meaning and apply what you learn to your life
4. Create a tool to help you remember what you learn
5. Extra Credit

1. Read the passage

Ephesians 6:10-17

> *Finally, be strong in the Lord and in his mighty power. Put on the full armor of God, so that you can take your stand against the devil's schemes. For our struggle is not against flesh and blood, but against the rulers, against the authorities, against the powers of this dark world and against the spiritual forces of evil in the heavenly realms. Therefore put on the full armor of God, so that when the*

day of evil comes, you may be able to stand your ground, and after you have done everything, to stand.

Stand firm then, with the belt[2] of truth buckled around your waist, with the breastplate of righteousness in place, and with your feet fitted with the readiness that comes from the gospel of peace.[3] In addition to all this, take up the shield of faith, with which you can extinguish all the flaming arrows of the evil one. Take the helmet of salvation[4] and the sword of the Spirit, which is the word of God.

2. Diagram or illustrate the concepts

Fill in the chart using Ephesians 6:10-13. (If you get stuck making the chart, see page 115 for suggestions.)

Spiritual Warfare in Ephesians 6:10-13

The Lord has...	The devil has...	Our opponents are...

- Draw your own soldier wearing the full armor of God. You may want to include the fiery darts.

3. Consider the meaning and apply what you learn

- Which pieces of armor are defensive and which offensive? What weapon(s) does God give us?
- How many times is the word "stand" used in the passage?[5] Think about what it means for a soldier to stand: to be at the ready for anything? to stand instead of run away or attack?
- Are you missing any components of your armor? What do you need to put on to ensure you can stand?
- What are some of the fiery darts aimed at you?
- Who is our struggle NOT against?
- Look back at Chapter 4. What does this soldier have in common with Jesus as he resisted the temptations of the devil in Matthew 4?
- Pray verses 14-17 on yourself right now.

4. Think of a creative way to teach the armor of God

- If you have young children, use cardboard or boxes to make a set of armor they can wear.
- Create a "paper doll soldier" kit.

Learning from the Early Christians

In the first chapters of this book we focused on using paper and pencil to bring *biblical stories* to life. In this second part of the book we are using similar techniques to deepen our understanding of *theological* or *teaching* sections of the Bible. We have looked at excerpts of letters written by the apostles Peter and Paul. The Book of Acts—which is actually "part two" of Luke's Gospel[6]—reveals the backstory of their lives and relates some of the experiences that informed their teachings.

Peter and Paul were both imprisoned for their faith and miraculously released in the middle of the night by unusual acts of God. They are inspiring examples of courageous "soldiers for the Lord" and their experiences of suffering resulted in wonderful advancements in the Kingdom of God.

1. Read the passages

Acts 4:1-4

> *The priests and the captain of the temple guard and the Sadducees came up to Peter and John while they were speaking to the people. They were greatly disturbed because the apostles were teaching the people, proclaiming in Jesus the resurrection of the dead. They seized Peter and John and, because it was evening, they put them in jail until the next day. But many who heard the message believed; so the number of men who believed grew to about five thousand.*

Acts 5:12-21, 40b-42

The apostles performed many signs and wonders among the people. And all the believers used to meet together in Solomon's Colonnade. No one else dared join them, even though they were highly regarded by the people Nevertheless, more and more men and women believed in the Lord and were added to their number. As a result, people brought the sick into the streets and laid them on beds and mats so that at least Peter's shadow might fall on some of them as he passed by. Crowds gathered also from the towns around Jerusalem, bringing their sick and those tormented by impure spirits, and all of them were healed.

Then the high priest and all his associates, who were members of the party of the Sadducees, were filled with jealousy. They arrested the apostles and put them in the public jail. But during the night an angel of the Lord opened the doors of the jail and brought them out. "Go, stand in the temple courts," he said, "and tell the people all about this new life."

At daybreak they entered the temple courts, as they had been told, and began to teach the people.

When the high priest and his associates arrived, they called together the Sanhedrin—the full assembly of the elders of Israel—and sent to the jail for the apostles.... They called the apostles in and had them flogged. Then they ordered them not to speak in the name of Jesus, and let them go.

The apostles left the Sanhedrin, rejoicing because they had been counted worthy of suffering disgrace for the Name. Day after day, in the temple courts and from house to house, they never stopped teaching and proclaiming the good news that Jesus is the Messiah.

Acts 12:1-17

It was about this time that King Herod arrested some who belonged to the church, intending to persecute them. He had James, the brother of John, put to death with the sword. When he saw that this met with approval among the Jews, he proceeded to seize Peter also. This happened during the Festival of Unleavened Bread. After arresting him, he put him in prison, handing him over to be guarded by four squads of *four soldiers each. Herod intended to bring him out for public trial after the Passover.*

So Peter was kept in prison, but the church was earnestly praying to God for him.

The night before Herod was to bring him to trial, Peter was sleeping between two soldiers, bound with two chains, and sentries stood guard at the entrance. Suddenly an angel of the Lord appeared and a light shone in the cell. He struck Peter on the side and woke him up. "Quick, get up!" he said, and the chains fell off Peter's wrists. Then the angel said to him, "Put on your clothes and sandals." And Peter did so.

"Wrap your cloak around you and follow me," the angel told him. Peter followed him out of the prison, but he had no idea that what the angel was doing was really happening; he thought he was seeing a vision. They passed the first and second guards and came to the iron gate leading to the city. It opened for them by itself, and they went through it. When they had walked the length of one street, suddenly the angel left him.

Then Peter came to himself and said, "Now I know without a doubt that the Lord has sent his angel and rescued me from Herod's clutches and from everything the Jewish people were hoping would happen."

When this had dawned on him, he went to the house of Mary the mother of John, also called Mark, where many people had gathered and were praying. Peter knocked at the outer entrance, and a servant named Rhoda came to answer the door. When she recognized Peter's voice, she was so overjoyed she ran back without opening it and exclaimed, "Peter is at the door!"

"You're out of your mind," they told her.

When she kept insisting that it was so, they said, "It must be his angel."

But Peter kept on knocking, and when they opened the door and saw him, they were astonished. Peter motioned with his hand for them to be quiet and described how the Lord had brought him out of prison. "Tell James and the other brothers and sisters about this," he said, and then he left for another place.

Acts 16:16-34

> Once when we were going to the place of prayer, we were
> met by a female slave who had a spirit by which she predicted
> the future. She earned a great deal of money for her owners by
> fortune-telling. She followed Paul and the rest of us, shouting,
> "These men are servants of the Most High God, who are
> telling you the way to be saved." She kept this up for many
> days. Finally Paul became so annoyed that he turned around
> and said to the spirit, "In the name of Jesus Christ I command
> you to come out of her!" At that moment the spirit left her.
>
> When her owners realized that their hope of making money
> was gone, they seized Paul and Silas and dragged them into
> the marketplace to face the authorities. They brought them
> before the magistrates and said, "These men are Jews, and
> are throwing our city into an uproar by advocating customs
> unlawful for us Romans to accept or practice."
>
> The crowd joined in the attack against Paul and Silas, and
> the magistrates ordered them to be stripped and beaten with
> rods. After they had been severely flogged, they were thrown
> into prison, and the jailer(was commanded to guard them
> carefully. When he received these orders, he put them in the
> inner cell and fastened their feet in the stocks.
>
> About midnight Paul and Silas were praying and singing
> hymns to God, and the other prisoners were listening to
> them. Suddenly there was such a violent earthquake that the
> foundations of the prison were shaken. At once all the prison
> doors flew open, and everyone's chains came loose. The jailer
> woke up, and when he saw the prison doors open, he drew
> his sword and was about to kill himself because he thought
> the prisoners had escaped. But Paul shouted, "Don't harm
> yourself! We are all here!"
>
> The jailer called for lights, rushed in and fell trembling
> before Paul and Silas. 30 He then brought them out and
> asked, "Sirs, what must I do to be saved?"
>
> They replied, "Believe in the Lord Jesus, and you will be
> saved—you and your household." 32 Then they spoke the
> word of the Lord to him and to all the others in his house.
> 33 At that hour of the night the jailer took them and washed

their wounds; then immediately he and all his household were baptized. 34 The jailer brought them into his house and set a meal before them; he was filled with joy because he had come to believe in God—he and his whole household.

2. Diagram the facts

Fill in the chart using the four passages from Acts. (If you get stuck making the chart, see pages 114-115 for suggestions.)

CHAPTER 6: **Christians in Prison in the Book of Acts** *(from pages 86-87)*

Who is in prison?	By whom?	Why?	
Acts 4			
Acts 5			
Acts 12			
Acts 16			

	How released?	Results

Use your imagination to put yourself in the situation of Acts 12. James, Peter's friend and fishing partner[7], has been beheaded. When Peter gets to the prayer meeting, they have trouble believing their prayers have been answered. How would you feel if you were Peter? Or the believers at John Mark's house?

In Acts 15, Paul and Silas were stripped and beaten with rods, a terrible punishment that tears the flesh. Then they were locked in the inner cell of the jail with their feet elevated and spread apart, fastened in stocks. How did they react? "About midnight Paul and Silas were praying and singing hymns to God, and the other prisoners were listening to them."

They did not weep and complain, instead they prayed and sang—and God miraculously set them free. In Paul's letter to the Philippians he tells them: "Rejoice in the Lord always. I will say it again: Rejoice!... I have learned the secret of being content in any and every situation.... I can do all things through him who gives me strength."

3. Consider the meaning for your life

Recently I spent a year living and studying in St Andrews, Scotland. In the Middle Ages St Andrews was a center of Christianity and many people from Europe made pilgrimage to its Cathedral overlooking the North Sea. St Andrews also became a site of much violence during the Protestant Reformation and several martyrs were executed in the town. One young man, Henry Forrest, particularly touches my heart because he was burned at the stake for reading from an English translation of the Bible.

How did the first Christians and the reformers (and many in between and since) handle their fear? Modern day neurologists says that the brain is wired so that it cannot be in a state of thankfulness and a state of fear at the same time.[8] Paul and Silas used singing to calm their fears and build their faith.

- Are their things connected to your faith that might get you in trouble?
- What or who might imprison you?
- How might God release you from what binds you?
- What results can you expect from your suffering?

4. Create tools to help you remember to be thankful

- Make a list of your favorite hymns and praise songs and write down the lyrics if you don't have them memorized.
- Keep a gratitude journal.

Facing Trials

Our next passage comes from the book of James. Traditionally, scholars believe James (along with the New Testament writer Jude) was one of the brothers of Jesus. While Jesus was alive, his brothers were skeptical of his ministry,[9] but after his resurrection, James became one of the leaders of the church in Jerusalem.[10]

The letter of James is a very practical book addressed to "the twelve tribes scattered among the nations." We learn from Acts 8:1 that after the stoning of Stephen, the first Christian martyr, "a great persecution broke out against the church in Jerusalem, and all except the apostles were scattered throughout Judea and Samaria." The people James is writing to are living in difficult situations. Like Paul in his letters, James stresses the importance of joy.

1. Read the passage

James 1:2-4

> *Consider it pure joy, my brothers and sisters, whenever you face trials of many kinds, because you know that the testing of your faith produces perseverance. Let*

perseverance finish its work so that you may be mature and complete, not lacking anything.

2. Diagram or illustrate the concepts

- Create your own pattern or design incorporating the progression of elements in James 1:2-4

trials → testing of faith → perseverance
→ mature & complete → joy

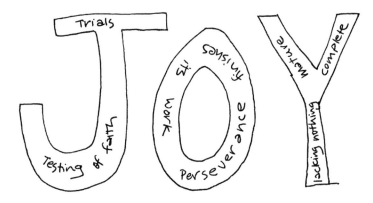

3. Consider the meaning and apply what you learn

- With what does James equate trials?
- What is the purpose of our trials?
- How can something difficult also be pure joy?
- Compare this passage to the thorny ground in the Parable of the Sower in chapter 1. How is joy an antidote to thorns?

4. Think of a creative way to remind yourself to rejoice

- Make a mobile of the word JOY.
- Make a braided wrist band.
- In one North African country, missionaries create henna tattoos with biblical images to teach Bible stories and remind believers of their faith.

5. Extra Credit

In the Book of Romans Paul describes a progression of elements similar to James, but Paul teaches how we can move from suffering to hope:

Romans 5:3-5

We also glory in our sufferings, because we know that suffering produces perseverance; perseverance, character; and character, hope. And hope does not put us to shame, because God's love has been poured out into our hearts through the Holy Spirit, who has been given to us.

- Illustrate this parallel passage which is parallel to James 1:2-4 and note any differences.

    suffering → perseverance → character → hope

CHAPTER 7

Holding onto Hope

A quick search on Google presents alarming statistics on depression. The Centers for Disease Control and Prevention estimated in March of 2011 that 10% of adults in the United States suffer from serious depression. An October 2011 report from online Canadian pharmacies reveals that Americans' use of antidepressant medication has increased 400% in the last two decades. They estimate that 11% of Americans aged twelve and over are taking antidepressant medication.

Even if not clinically diagnosed with depression, many of us limp through days of sadness and despair. I do. Years ago a wise counselor gave me insight into my own bouts of depression. I had heard that depression was often suppressed anger. She told me depression could be any unexpressed emotion and suggested that perhaps my feelings of despair were connected to loss.

Since then, when I feel despondent and a heaviness weighs me down, I ask myself if I have lost something—a person, a place, an object, a dream? Amazingly this thought often lifts the grip of depression so that I'm able to take action and move toward hope.

But how do we gain an attitude of hope? In the last chapter we saw biblical writers claim that joy follows from trials and hope from suffering. How is this possible? What is the source of hope?

1. Read the passage
2. Diagram or illustrate the concepts
3. Consider the meaning and apply what you learn to your life
4. Think of creative ways to share what you've learned with others
5. Extra credit

Unseen Resources

Although I was not brought up in a Christian home and had little contact with the Bible, there were many positive influences in my life. One of my favorite books is *McElligot's Pool*, an early work of Dr. Seuss. In the story a little boy is fishing when a farmer tells him he will never catch anything in such a small pool. But in the boy's big imagination the pool might be connected to an underground brook—and river—and then connect with the sea. If he is patient enough he might catch any number of things.

Think back on your own childhood: perhaps there are influences that contribute to your interests and your outlook on life today.

When I read the first chapter of Paul's letter to the Colossians, I was struck by the verb he uses to describe the connection between faith, hope, and love. He says faith and love "spring" from hope. In the margin of my Bible, using my special micro pen[1] that does not bleed through paper, I drew two flowers, "faith and love", springing up from a clump of "hope".

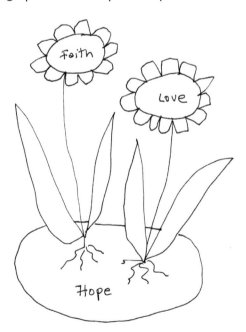

But when I looked more closely, I noticed that hope is not described as something growing up from the earth, but our hope is "stored up in heaven." So I made a more comprehensive drawing, showing the flow of hope from heaven, down to us through our faith in Christ Jesus and our love for all God's people. Then hope spreads into the whole world where it is bearing fruit. According to this passage, hope is not something that originates in us, but something we receive from an infinite supply that is kept safe for us in heaven. We access hope today by exercising faith and expressing love.

1. Read the passage

Colossians 1:3-6

> *We always thank God, the Father of our Lord Jesus Christ, when we pray for you, because we have heard of your faith in Christ Jesus and of the love you have for all his people— the faith and love that spring from the hope stored up for you in heaven and about which you have already heard in the true word of the gospel that has come to you. In the same way, the gospel is bearing fruit and growing throughout the whole world— just as it has been doing among you since the day you heard it and truly understood God's grace.*

- What do you put your faith/confidence/trust/reliance in?
- According to this passage, how do we learn about the hope stored up in heaven?
- Have you "truly understood God's grace"?
- How might theses ideas help you when you feel hopeless and discouraged?

2. Diagram or illustrate the concepts

Take a second look at the passage. Underline key words. Let yourself "doodle" or make a schematic drawing that helps you unpack, understand, and remember these important truths.

3. Consider the meaning for your life

Who are people you thank God for in your prayers? Send them a letter, email, or text message expressing your thanks for them.

4. Think of a creative way to share what you've learned with others

Make a card with your own design of these verses and post in on Instagram or Pinterest.

Put a map of the world on your refrigerator and add photos or stories of good things happening around the world.

Security in Christ

Not only do I have days when I struggle with depression, but I have had nights when dreams frightened me so much that I woke up in a state of panic. The images and stories welling up from my subconscious (or perhaps enter my sleeping mind through subliminal talking from the enemy) seemed so real that my body was thrown into fight or flight mode and I had trouble getting control of my thoughts. I felt lost or frozen or trapped in a darkness without God.

On those occasions, I had to get out of bed and walk into another room. Sometimes the most I could do was call on the name of Jesus. And he came to me. I sensed a crack of light and grabbed hold of a memory of one of his promises: *The Lord is my shepherd. I will never leave you or forsake you. I am the beginning and the end.* God's Word rescued me because it was a lifeline from his being directly into my mind.

Many years ago a young man knocked on our door and asked if we needed our roof re-shingled. We got to talking and I realized Tom (as I will call him) was living in the cab of his shabby pickup truck. I invited him to sleep in our basement. As Tom observed the life of our church and our worship of Jesus, he said he liked a lot of elements of Christianity, but not the exclusivity of Jesus as the only way to God. He himself followed an Indian guru named Sai Baba. Tom set up an altar in our basement complete with a photograph of Sai Baba.[2] Despite many conversations and prayers, Tom was not persuaded to follow Christ and after a month or so he moved to another state where there was a community of Sai Baba worshippers.

Not long afterwards I was surprised to get a phone call

from Tom. He told me the Sai Baba community practiced long hours of silent meditation. One member who called himself "Freedom" never talked, but people liked to meditate near him because he was so "spiritual".

One day Freedom was meditating and left his body and went to another realm.[3] While in this disembodied state, he was visited by Sai Baba who wanted to take over his body. Apparently this was painful and Freedom didn't want to be possessed, so he called out for help. In desperation he called on the name of Jesus- and guess what? Jesus showed up! He freed Freedom from Sai Baba, Freedom went back into his body in the meditation room, and told everyone who was Lord!

Tom relayed this metaphor from Freedom: there are many moons, but only one sun. We must worship the source of light and not the reflection of it. That day Tom and many others became followers of the one true God, Jesus Christ.

1. Read the passage

Romans 8:32b-39

> *If God is for us, who can be against us? He who did not spare his own Son, but gave him up for us all—how will he not also, along with him, graciously give us all things? Who will bring any charge against those whom God has chosen? It is God who justifies. Who then is the one who condemns? No one. Christ Jesus who died—more than that, who was raised to life—is at the right hand of God and is also interceding for us. Who shall separate us from the love of Christ? Shall trouble or hardship or persecution or famine or nakedness or danger or sword?*
>
> *As it is written:*
>
>> *"For your sake we face death all day long;*
>> *we are considered as sheep to be slaughtered."*
>
> *No, in all these things we are more than conquerors through him who loved us. For I am convinced that neither*

death nor life, neither angels nor demons, neither the present nor the future, nor any powers, neither height nor depth, nor anything else in all creation, will be able to separate us from the love of God that is in Christ Jesus our Lord.

2. Diagram or illustrate the concepts

Here is my drawing of the passage. Make one of your own.

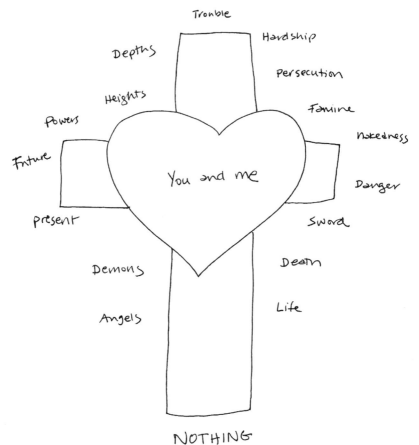

3. Consider the meaning of the text and apply what you learn

- Make a list in your own words of things that threaten to separate you from God's love.
- Are there things that DO separate you now? How can you change that?

4. Think of something you can make to remind you of your unshakable security in Christ

- Cut out a design from colored cellophane and use spray glue to make a "stained glass" window in your house.
- Find an interesting stone and place it somewhere in your home or office as an "ebenezer"—a stone to remember that God is your help.[4]

5. Extra credit

Compare the Romans passage to Paul's personal list below.

2 Corinthians 11:23b-33

I have worked much harder, been in prison more frequently, been flogged more severely, and been exposed to death again and again. Five times I received from the Jews the forty lashes minus one. Three times I was beaten with rods, once I was pelted with stones, three times I was shipwrecked, I spent a night and a day in the open sea, I have been constantly on the move. I have been in danger from rivers, in danger from bandits, in danger from my fellow Jews, in danger from Gentiles; in danger in the city, in danger in the country, in danger at sea; and in danger from false believers. I have labored and toiled and have often gone without sleep; I have known hunger and thirst and have often gone without food. I have been cold and naked. Besides everything else, I face daily the pressure of my concern for all the churches.... In Damascus the governor under King Aretas had the city of the Damascenes guarded in order to arrest me. But I was lowered in a basket from a window in the wall and slipped through his hands.[5]

• make your own list of personal trials

God's Forever Promise

In the last two chapters we have been looking at Scripture passages that help us thrive as joyful and hope-filled Christians in this world. The writers give us practical advice and rational explanations of what it means to live like Jesus. But from its beginning in Genesis to its end in Revelation, the Bible is not afraid to address the BIG questions of life: where did we come from and where are we going? What existed before time began and what happens to us when we die?

Many parts of the Bible mention the creation and re-creation of the earth. Scholars vary widely in interpreting of these passages. Revelation is full of eschatology[6] and is one of the hardest books of the Bible to understand. The frightening images and the dream-like quality of the story keep many people from reading it —even though it begins with a promise: *"Blessed is the one who reads the words of this prophecy, and blessed are those who hear it and take to heart what is written in it, because the time is near."*

Several years ago I studied Revelation and made sketches of many of the scenes in John's vision. I compiled those images into one large (5' x 7') painting. That painting became the basis of a 45-minute video on Revelation[7]. My goal was not to interpret the meaning of John's prophecy, but to see what the text actually said and engrave it on my heart and mind. I believe that much of biblical prophecy is given to us so that when the events happen we can look back and see that God's words are trustworthy and true. Fulfilled prophecy strengthens our faith and helps us trust what is yet to come.

A helpful principle in studying the Bible is to let the text interpret itself. So in Revelation I paid attention to repeating phrases and themes, and to instances where the angel speaking to John tells him what something means. Because I am studying the Bible visually, I often find images repeating from one book to another. When I painted the Gospel of Mark, I noticed that the way Jesus talks about the end times in the Olivet Discourse[8] has a lot of overlap with John's vision in Revelation.

A passage in the end of Peter's second letter caught my eye because of the visual elements he uses. Here is my picture of Peter's teaching about the history—past and future—of the earth.

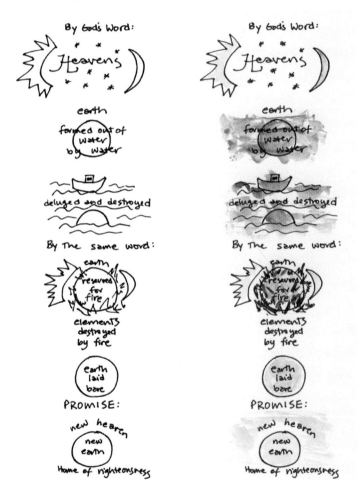

1. Read the passage

2 Peter 3:1-10

>Dear friends, this is now my second letter to you. I have written both of them as reminders to stimulate you to wholesome thinking. I want you to recall the words spoken in the past by the holy prophets and the command given by our Lord and Savior through your apostles.
>
>Above all, you must understand that in the last days scoffers will come, scoffing and following their own evil desires. They will say, "Where is this 'coming' he promised? Ever since our ancestors died, everything goes on as it has since the beginning of creation." But they deliberately forget that long ago by God's word the heavens came into being and the earth was formed out of water and by water. By these waters also the world of that time was deluged and destroyed. By the same word the present heavens and earth are reserved for fire, being kept for the day of judgment and destruction of the ungodly.
>
>But do not forget this one thing, dear friends: With the Lord a day is like a thousand years, and a thousand years are like a day. The Lord is not slow in keeping his promise, as some understand slowness. Instead he is patient with you, not wanting anyone to perish, but everyone to come to repentance.
>
>But the day of the Lord will come like a thief. The heavens will disappear with a roar; the elements will be destroyed by fire, and the earth and everything done in it will be laid bare.

- As you read this letter, put yourself in the place of the first readers. What is the tone of the letter?
- What does Peter want us to remember—or not forget?
- What do to the scoffers deliberately forget?
- Notice the frequent use of "word." How important is God's Word in your life?

2. Diagram or illustrate the passage

- Make a timeline that incorporates all the ideas Peter wants us to remember.

3. Think of a creative way to apply the principles to your own life

My most recent visual Bible study and painting was of the life of Abraham. I read through Genesis 12-22 and sketched 66 scenes from his life. At the same time I was auditing a class on covenants at St Mary's Divinity School in St Andrews, Scotland. My professor often remarked on the "roller coaster" pattern of Abraham's journey of faith. One of the benefits of looking intently into a whole biblical narrative and not just a small segments is the perspective you gain. Abraham did not just "happen" to have faith strong enough to be able to offer his son Isaac as a sacrifice to God; he had years of experiencing God's promises, then his own failures, and his recovery back to a stronger faith. His trials made his faith stronger and his hope secure.

- Make a timeline of your own life: where you came from and where you are going.
- Include early influences—people, books, experiences—that contribute to your personality and passions.
- Note the ups and downs in your relationship with God and his Word. Do you see any patterns?
- What are some of your hopes for your future here on earth?
- Where do you see yourself after this life ends?

How Do We Become Like Jesus?

"You will receive power when the Holy Spirit comes on you; and you will be my witnesses in Jerusalem, and in all Judea and Samaria, and to the ends of the earth." —Acts 1:8

CHAPTER 8

Continuing on Your Own

I you have enjoyed the exercises in this book and will continue to meditate on and "digest" the Bible by combining your rational left-brain study with creative, right-brain expressions. Consider collecting supplies such as your Bible, pens, sketchbook, pencils, pencil sharpener, eraser, colored pencils, pastels, watercolors, modeling clay, and store them in a box or bag. Set aside a special nook or corner in your house where you can work and pray.

You can start by choosing a topic:
- A Cure for Worry: *Philippians 4:4-7*
- The Gifts of the Spirit: *1 Corinthians 12:7-11*
- The True Nature of Love: *1 Corinthians 13:4-8*
- The Purpose of the Bible: *2 Timothy 3:16-17*
- What God's Word Can Do: *Hebrews 4:12-13*
- What Love Looks Like: *Romans 12:9-21*

Or exploring a short passage:
- *Genesis 1:1-2:3*
- *Psalm 23*
- *Isaiah 6:1-7*
- *Ezekiel 1*
- *Malachi 4:1-3*

Once you get a taste for this method of interacting with God's Word, you might like to tackle a larger project. I am in the middle of studying/sketching/painting scenes from the Gospel of John and am discovering many insights into the text. I am painting on 3' x 3' canvas and as I approach each new day of painting, I reread the whole passage and keep finding things I missed! This is truly a *visual lectio divina* for me.

Some projects I'd like to work on in the future are:
- The life of Joseph
- The life of Moses
- The life of John the Baptist
- Women of the Bible

As you delve into the lives of biblical characters, sketching their experiences and painting their expressions, don't be surprised if you find yourself making an emotional connection with them. The Bible is not an academic text book but stories of real people who knew and loved and served the same God we worship today. Jesus Christ is the same yesterday, today, and forever.

Completed Chart Samples

CHAPTER 1: **Jesus Teaches about Four Types of Soil** *(from page 28)*

A. Path	B. Rocks
Satan takes away the Word	Joy / Persecution + Troubles => Fall Away
C. Thorns	**D. Good Soil**
Worries Wealth Desires > Choke => Unfruitful	Hear + Accept => 30, 60, 100

CHAPTER 2: **Jesus Calms the Storm** *(from page 39)*

Jesus	Natural World	Disciples
"Let us go over to the other side."		*They took Jesus in the boat just as he was.*
Jesus was in the stern, sleeping on a cushion.	*A furious squall nearly swapped the boat.*	*They were afraid. They woke Jesus and said, "Don't you care if we drown?"*
He got up, rebuked the wind, and said to the waves, "Quiet! Be still!"	*The wind died down. It was completely calm.*	*They were terrified.*
"Why are you so afraid? Do you still have no faith?"		*"Who is this? Even the wind and the waves obey him!"*

CHAPTER 4: **Jesus is Tested in the Wilderness** *(from pages 60-61)*

Scene	Speaker or Actor	Situation	
1	A voice from heaven	*Jesus is baptized. The Spirit of God descends on him like a dove.*	
2	The Spirit		
3	Tempter	*Jesus fasts 40 days and nights and is hungry.*	
	Jesus		
4	The devil	*Took Jesus to the holy city and had him stand on the highest point of the temple.*	
	Jesus		
5	The devil	*Took Jesus to a very high mountain and showed him all the kingdoms of the world and their splendor.*	
	Jesus		
6	Angels	*The devil left Jesus.*	

CHAPTER 3: Jesus Feeds the 4,000 and 5,000 (from page 52)

	Mark 6:30-45	Mark 8:1-11
Where does the feeding take place?	Galilee—the west side of the lake	Decapolis—the east side of the lake
How does Jesus feel toward the people?	Compassion: they are like sheep without a shepherd	Compassion: they might collapse on their way home
How much food does Jesus start with?	Five loaves, two fish	Seven loaves, a few small fish
How much food is left over?	Twelve basketfuls	Seven basketfuls
How many people were fed?	5,000 men	4,000 people

Words Spoken or Actions Taken	Reference
"This is my Son, whom I love; with him I am well pleased."	
Led Jesus into the desert.	
"If you are the Son of God, tell these stones to become bread."	
"It is written: People do not live on bread alone, but on every word that comes from the mouth of God."	Deut. 8:3
"If you are the Son of God, throw yourself down, for it is written: 'He will command his angels concerning you, and they will lift you up in their hands, so that you will not strike your foot against a stone.'"	Psalm 91:11,12
"It is also written: 'Do not put the Lord your God to the test.'"	Deut. 6:16
"All this I will give you if you will bow down and worship me."	
"Away from me, Satan! For is is written: 'Worship the Lord your God, and serve him only.'"	Deut. 6:13
They attended to Jesus.	

CHAPTER 5: **Attitudes and Actions in 2 Peter 1:5-7** (from page 71)

Attitude	Action
Faith	Goodness
Knowledge	Self-control
Perseverance	Godliness
Mutual affection	Love

CHAPTER 6: **Christians in Prison in the Book of Acts** (from pages 88-89)

Who is in prison?	By whom?	Why?	
Acts 4 Peter and John	Priests, captain of the temple guard, Sadducees	Teaching about the resurrection	
Acts 5 Apostles	High priest, Sadducess	Miracles, signs and wonders, many hearings, jealousy	
Acts 12 Peter (James had been killed)	King Herod	To persecute Christians and to please Jews	
Acts 16 Paul and Silas	Magistrates in Philippi	Owners of slave girl lost money after Paul sent her evil spirit away	

CHAPTER 6: **Spiritual Warfare in Ephesians 6:10-13** *(from page 82)*

The Lord has...	The devil has...	Our opponents are...
Mighty power	Schemes	Rulers
Full armor	Day of evil	Authorities
		Powers of this dark world
		Spiritual forces of evil in the heavenly realms

How released?	Results
Rulers, elders, teachers of the law (Sanhedrin)	Many believed—5,000 men.
Angel	Flogging, rejoicing
Angel	Answer to prayer
Earthquake (singing?)	Jailer and his family believed and were baptized

Sample Symbols

water   boat   sun   moon

God on the Throne

Scroll

angel   King   Queen

man   woman
        with
        baby

sitting

Elders

Pharisees

Saducees

old man

Jesus

John The Baptist

angel

High Priest

Soldier

magician

Satan, the devil

synagogue

house

mountains

empty tomb

demons

cross

Endnotes

Introduction

[1] L'Abri is a French word meaning shelter. L'Abri Fellowship is a Christian Study Center in Switzerland founded by Francis and Edith Schaeffer.

[2] Just a few verses later in a Acts 23:23 I had to draw the 200 soldiers, 70 horsemen, and 200 spearmen who escorted Paul to Caesarea.

[3] *Lectio Divina* is a traditional Christian practice of scriptural reading, meditation, and prayer intended to promote communion with God and to increase knowledge of God's Word. It does not treat Scripture as a text to be studied, but as the Living Word with Christ as the key to its meaning. The monastic practice of *Lectio Divina* was first established in the 6th century by Saint Benedict.

CHAPTER 1: Jesus is the Word of God

[1] Matthew 4:4

[2] 1 Peter 2:2; 1 Corinthians 3:12; Hebrews 5:12

[3] Psalm 19:7-11

[4] Romans 12:2

[5] 2 Timothy 4:16-17

[6] Matthew 13:1-23; Luke 8:4-15. An easy way to compare passages in the gospels is to consult a "Synopsis of the Four Gospels" where the verses are laid out in parallel. Or look up the passage on the internet at a site such as BibleGateway.com and choose "add a parallel."

[7] Don't worry, no one is going to grade you. These are related passages you might want to do on your own.

[8] If you need help, see Sample Symbols on pages 117-120 in the back of this book.

CHAPTER 2: Jesus is Lord of Creation

[1] There are simple tests on the Internet that help you figure out if you are more right or left brained. www.intelliscript.net/test_area/questionnaire/questionnaire.cgi

[2] The Greek word used here for cushion only occurs this once in the whole Bible. The term means "cushion for the head" but was also used in a boat as a rower's cushion. Why is this important? Because details like this point to the presence of an eye witness. Mark's gospel has several such details and many scholars believe Mark got his information straight from the disciple Peter.

[3] Not to confuse you, but another reference book speculates that the cushion is probably a sandbag used for ballast—either a sack of 100-120 pounds, or a pillow of 50 pounds. The important insight is the presence of an eyewitness!

[4] See parallels in Matthew 14:22-32 and John 6:16-21.

CHAPTER 3: Jesus is Lord over Evil

[1] The "lake" mentioned in Mark's gospel is called by various names in the Bible. Most commonly we think of it as the Sea of Galilee, but it is also called the Sea of Tiberias in John 21:1, the Lake of Gennesaret in Luke 5:1, and the Sea of Kinnereth in Numbers 34:11 and Joshua 12:3. Since the Bible was written thousands of years ago, it is not unusual to find a range of names for one geographical location. Scholars try to pinpoint locations, but often the name no longer exists.

[2] Some manuscripts call this region Gadarenes, others Gergesenes. It is interesting to note that our text only mentions Jesus getting out of the boat. Is it possible the disciples didn't set foot on the pagan soil?

[3] The steep slope would be closer to the lake if the water level was higher.

[4] Isaiah 35:5-6 lists four miraculous signs that will happen when the Messiah comes: the blind will see, the deaf will hear, the lame will leap like a deer, and the mute will shout for joy.

[5] A note about the feeding of the 5000. Except for the Resurrection of Jesus, this is the only miracle of Jesus recorded in all four gospels. Although the text does not state the location of this event, scholars generally agree that this took place somewhere in Galilee, probably on the southwest shore. See Matthew 14:13-21, Luke 9:10-17, and John 6:1-13.

CHAPTER 4: Jesus is the Son of God

[1] I have a funny story. Not long after I came home from Switzerland and my encounter with the Living God, I was invited to a party with friends from my junior high days. I was 21 and could legally drink, but I wasn't sure what God wanted me to do, so I prayed about it. As it turned out, a family who were leaders in Intervarsity Christian Fellowship invited me to dinner that same night, before the party. At the table they read Psalm 60. I didn't see the words;

I just heard them say, "you give us wine to make us real." Oh, I thought, this is an answer to my prayer. If I have a glass of wine, it might help me be more real to my friends—and I'll be able to tell them about Jesus. I went to the party, I had a little wine even though I don't like it, and God arranged some good conversations. Was I surprised months later when I happened on Psalm 60 in my Bible. The whole of verse 3 says, "You have shown your people desperate times; you have given us wine that makes us reel." In his goodness and mercy, even though I had misunderstood, God blessed me.

[2] Matthew, Mark, and Luke are called the Synoptic Gospels because they include many of the same stories of Jesus' life, often in the same sequence. Some scholars believe Mark, the shortest of the three, was written first, and that Matthew and Luke may have read and used Mark as an outline. John, on the other hand, takes a unique approach.

[3] The Temple in Jerusalem was 150 feet (15 stories) high.

[4] Alcoholics Anonymous has an acronym to help people recognize signs of vulnerability: HALT—Hungry, Angry, Lonely, Tired.

[5] Isaiah 43:19; Revelation 21:5

CHAPTER 5: Growing in God

[1] 2 Corinthians 11:23-29

[2] Philippians 4:11-13

[3] Philippians 4:4

[4] The Greek word translated as witchcraft is *pharmakeia*, the root word for pharmacy.

CHAPTER 6: Living in the World

[1] Metaphor—"pictures in words"—are often good candidates for creating a visual study aid.

[2] The Greek actually says "wrap truth around your loins (private parts)". We need truth next to our skin.

[3] Isaiah 52:7 "How beautiful on the mountains are the feet of those who bring good news."

[4] 1 Thessalonians 5:8 "Put on faith and love as a breastplate, and the hope of salvation as a helmet."

[5] Pay close attention to repeated words; that is a clue to what the author considers most important.

[6] Both Luke and Acts begin by addressing Theophilus. In Greek this name means "God lover". Theophilus could have been an actual person—or a stand-in for all of us.

CHAPTER 7: Holding on to Hope

[1] I love to use "Micron" fine tip pens manufactured by Sakura. They allow me to underline, circle words, make notes and doodle in my Bible without bleeding through the paper. It's also fun to record dates of important events in your life and notes from sermons and teachings—to create a "Bible Memoir".

[2] Before I became a Christian I was briefly involved in Transcendental Meditation and was familiar with this sort of altar to a human being. I have fully renounced all such practices!

[3] This sort of thing is hard for many of us to comprehend, but compare this with what Paul writes in 2 Corinthians 12:2-4.

[4] See 1 Samuel 7:12, "Then Samuel took a stone and set it up between Mizpah and Shen. He named it Ebenezer, saying, 'Thus far the Lord has helped us.'" Also see the lyrics to "Come Thou Fount of Every Blessing".

[5] You can read the stories of many of the experiences Paul lists here in the Book of Acts.

[6] Eschatology means the study of the last things, the end times, the end of the world as we know it now.

[7] My video, *Painting Revelation*, includes a 6-week study on Revelation with charts and exercises similar to the ones in this book. You can download it for free from my website: debbytopliff.com.

[8] Not long before Jesus is arrested, Peter and Andrew and James and John ask him what is going to happen in the future. It's called the Olivet Discourse, or teaching, because they were sitting on the Mount of Olives—an olive grove. All three of the synoptic gospels relate this teaching. Mark 13:3-27; Matthew 24:3-31; Luke 21:8-28.

Debby Topliff
Visual Translations of the Bible

Debby Topliff is a painter and teacher with creative gifts that
make the stories of the Bible come alive. She creates large-scale
paintings based on her in-depth study of whole books of the
Bible. Her unique talent for teaching takes you on a visual journey
through the painting that is a map leading the viewer to a rich
understanding of the story.

Debby discovered the joy of painting later in life when she realized it was a vehicle for visual storytelling. After overcoming her inhibition of being a self-taught, naif artist, she embraced the medium and began to create vivid, childlike paintings based her studies. She paints in the tradition of early Christian art—with a modern, playful twist - using bright colors and a primitive style that present the biblical narrative in an inviting, multicultural format.

Recent works include the Gospel of Mark, Acts of the Apostles, the Life of Abraham, and the Book of Revelation. Her painting of Revelation is the basis of an ALA award-winning, 45-minute video, "Painting Revelation." It retells the story of the complex book of Revelation in a way that makes its message accessible and understandable. Copies of her DVD are available from Christian Book Distributors or may be downloaded from her website.

Debby's painting flows from her heart, the heart of a teacher. Her gifts become evident as you listen to her explain her art and tell the stories that inspire her. She welcomes opportunities to give talks and workshops to groups of all ages, sizes, and faith traditions.

Debby received a BA from the University of Michigan and an MA from Trinity Evangelical Divinity School. She is the mother of three, grandmother of six, and lives with her husband near Lake Michigan.

Stunning full-size cloth reproductions of Debby's paintings are available as teaching tools for churches and mission groups. Contact Debby for more information and visit her website.

DEBBYTOPLIFF.COM   debbytopliff@gmail.com

9299641R00072

Printed in Great Britain
by Amazon.co.uk, Ltd.,
Marston Gate.